Presidents

Mary Kate Bolinder

Presidents have many jobs.

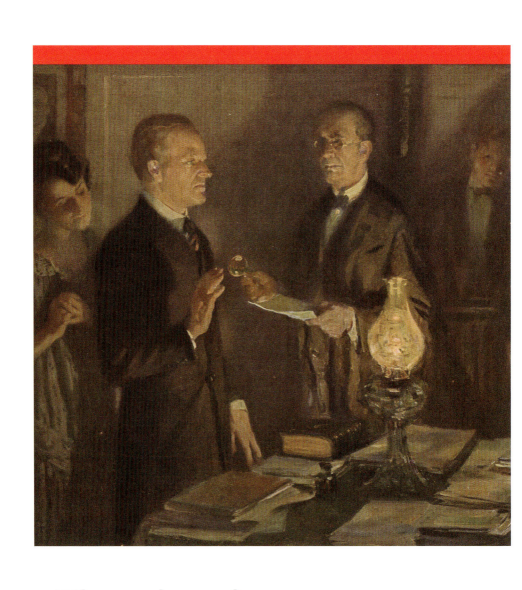

They lead us.

They work from the White House.

Think and Talk

Where else does the president work?

They help make laws.

They make speeches.

They lead our troops.

They help people in
need.

The president works
for all of us.

Jump into Fiction

Dream Big

Nina has a big dream.

She wants to be president.

Civics in Action

The president does many things. You can help others learn about the job of the president.

1. Think about what the president does.

2. Make a poster of one job the president does.

3. Share your poster with others.